put together to have a place

ANTHONY GENTILE

Antonius Selection

To imaginary friends,
where are you, Ink
I miss you

PUT TOGETHER TO HAVE A PLACE

ONE

It starts with the breath
such a simple thing
convicted free convicted
I am trying to be better
less me
It's hard to make sense out of nothing
so
many don't
I try
I can almost see a tree
I remember our house
or at least the words
almost a tree
thoughts before life and death
or sleep

It can't be one big story
if it were
I wouldn't exist

TWO

surrounding and closing in
is your body
the size of a shut door

I pray
still ink
in your shape
a remaining blot
night wrought with grief
outline of everything I lost
all that matters
I plead with God
then blacker
Cerberus growls
so I stop
but I don't die
I keep stopping
and I don't die

THREE

where was he
our father
where was he
do not say he was there
that he saw
that he let man kill man
for thinking they could be father
because he told them
they could be father
who would want to be father
if he was there
if he saw
that he let man kill man
for thinking they could be father
and so on and so on

FOUR

she has many faces
and knows none of them

she plays the piano on her knees
finishing Mozart

in between
she balances
always about to fall

she must blink when I blink
or her eyes never close
two earths
under wings of complete obedience
unlike mine and unlike yours

she came to me in a dream
and stayed after I awoke

she stays

FIVE

I cannot speak of horror or love
all I know is confusion
sand falling through my fingers
gravity is against me
I want to be someone else
someone not glass
I could collapse
from the smallest breeze
from your breath
people are supposed to bend
but something's stuck
the punchline never comes
I'm waiting to laugh
it's the only thing I haven't let go of
everyone is dead
their words under the water
where we bathed as cherubs

SIX

I don't want her
I don't want this

there are no mirrors
the world scared of vanity
no corners
each person is a circle
each room is a web
I can't get out
not with that look
like I would be food
if I wasn't poisonous
I'm sorry God
I can't cut my hands off
I still kiss your feet
life is a gift
I see that
but
it's either not enough
or too much

I can't take it

the sound of sin being
so loud
wheels turning
screeching

SEVEN

what's that thing that I feel
a song or movement
shadowy dancer
bending like a birch
and then a willow

she's fallen
broke her ankle

I try to help her
she wants nothing to do with me

so I choose another thing
this one I know
a child of nonsense
deceiving
and saving me
a sip of soda

EIGHT

the words are a person
sometimes a mob
born after amen
at first breath
their light dims
to a harsh final flickering
like lovers do to trees
they scratch into my skull
with their dull pocket knife
"Not me!"
"Don't be me!"
then there's the things
seen in less than a second
half images
and there's a sound
a whistle
and a taste
of plastic or paper
a smell unannounced
rudely intruding
strangers on a bus

I always thought I had too many days
really they are all only things
and I am just a box
tearing
about to collapse

NINE

sun crown

sleek armor

feast smile

hands crushing coffee beans

young white strands of hair
carefully placed according to chaos
a gentleman's choice of wild

eyes of new
telling the time
when war has passed

arms a fleet of horses

words paint and heat
without the weight of sense
so we float
in us are bread and wine

his throne is a wooden chair
seated at the table
on the cliff
looking over the water
under the tree
where we remember
hurting only in laughter

TEN

uglier than a sergeant
the same cloth hangs tamely on clocked skin
every finger spills out of their mouth

years melt into chocolates
on pretzel sticks
I can only taste the dry

I forgot to move
when they moved

the wood support beam
instructed to curl and twist
like tiger lily petals
snap
stabbing through my back
becoming a fifth limb

the grass grows in patches
there could be a demon in any corner
And my office chair can't swivel anymore
I stay away from smoke
but dust fills my lungs

I've tuned out everything nonessential
so I can't hear you
only a cello
I'm on the floor

I didn't forget

ELEVEN

her hair is in her eyes
silk blacker
than her leather jacket

singing not music
something new
staining the air
stinging open skin

fighting out of her stone
it's clear the pleading sound
is not her own
she almost scared off beauty
sentenced to this

I am shards of glass on the floor of the palace
she picks me up
with her hands

TWELVE

the bureau had me
usually it's the floor
at best the dust floating in the lamplight
but my mom was in the room
I didn't know why

I pretended she wasn't
I pretended that I wasn't
like how I am

so I played
moving the draws
fiddling with the handles

a snowball hits my window
my friends beg for a soldier

I stayed inside
wondering why there wasn't a word
an explanation
then I thought
there is one
but I will never know it
be able to give it a name
I will only ever watch it
slip
water off a window

THIRTEEN

do you forget simple words
and do some loiter
like love
love

I puke out my spine
to have something to eat
still I need more

strike me like a match
all wet from the rain
shut my eyes with a baseball bat

I'm tired
failing the test of trick answers
multiple choice
A to Z to hieroglyphs
the trick being everything is right

bones I think
perish
I thought

FOURTEEN

my thumb has their pulse
I put them to my lips
try to whisper something discouraging
what I do with my hands
strangle evolution
squeeze worms
bruise bananas
tell them
I only talk when no one's around
and I get loud

I make myself out of clay
out of spite
and they
animate
try to make a person
they think it helps
I need more than a rib

FIFTEEN

grant good night
but not before so many setting suns
I'm told they rise too
there is more than waiting
the sky conceptualized
can't count all my thoughts
and twice that feelings
some things are infinite
long broad strokes
needing and having
our body

I've looked at you for so long
that now
I see my face

SIXTEEN

I knew this when I was eight
crying in an empty dog pen
other kids hitting each other with sticks in the woods

there are no demons
or angels
simply God
a heart irregularly beating

lead persuades poison
painter's tape stops the bleeding

I'm all out of ideas
but I keep seeing her
my sons and daughter
haunting
screaming against the air
that they are not the same
another's breath
they do this
over and over
more than I allow
never fully convincing themselves

SEVENTEEN

in sawing off my limbs
beneath a canopy
branches were reaching and bowing
and I thought
we are the same
but you look back
when I follow
and I can tell you want me to turn around

the last leg took every image of you
all I could remember

and

life is easier

EIGHTEEN

I used to look at the door
and see you there
feet off the ground

the yellow paint comes off in the rain
off a rusting frame
of the gilded sun

smiles have melted
real women permanently formed
a frown of understanding

no more opinions
no beliefs
there is nothing I stand for

as with any novel
I won't remember you
not your hair waving goodbye as you left
intangible harp strings

that empty space

NINETEEN

see how they live
I could never do that

there's a melody in their thinking
that I would like to hear
but they keep talking over it

so I make the corner strange
remaining uninhabited

king peasant jester drunkard knight squire
to no kingdom

there were so many flowers on the path
I had to walk on them
many of them
I won't do that again

TWENTY

I hide in hatred
because I didn't grab a rose
I didn't want to pluck it from the earth

I carry around dirt in my pocket
obsessed with my ashes

I want to snap their bones
like I was a Boy Scout
breaking sticks over my knee

I am not them
I do not grow with the sun
I hide in hatred

there's scratching at the door
a loud fit of madness
lack of fear
lapse of common consideration

still
only scratches

TWENTY-ONE

while writing you a letter
all of my insides fell out
I have to pick them up from the ground
now there's dog hair in my liver
and my heart has some splinters
from the damn broken-up hardwood floor
of my bedroom
that I can't leave
because these organs are so heavy
I cannot simply lift them with my hands
and if I could
if I put them into their place
how do I get them to stay
to withstand such abuse
when death so entices
and them having no idea
how vital they are

TWENTY-TWO

all I have is on a train
in a museum
closed last century

I dug into the earth
and lost my hands along the way

there might be a heaven
but I chose beauty
and choose beauty to be
the things I cannot have
any person
anyone but me

permanent dirt
on teeth
clothes and hair

notes hide the walls
I fall past stars
The whole blanket
always expecting to see someone
a hand
my first love
and last love

TWENTY-THREE

there's a surge I breathe in
at the escape of your name
it is what makes each step
seeing you moves everything else
be still
kind
each glance only brings me a small distance
wear your hair different
and I'll go further
time takes time
takes me
I want to live
stop moving

I needed an extra poem

but I've got nothing

and so you get this

I try to make things fair

I believe it is our duty

and here I willingly fail

although

how can we be more

than what there is

yet again

this exists

a page to fit the count

language all over again